ISBN 978-0-578-58389-1
Library of Congress Control Number: 2019915336
Rich Real Estate Legend Of The Flip Your 5 Laws
By: Daryl Haskins

Dedication
I dedicate this book to my children! You are and will always be GREAT. Keep moving forward and complete your goals.

TABLE OF CONTENTS

A WORD FROM THE AUTHOR

◆ ◆ ◆

Organized planning is to know exactly what to do with your money, time, health and vision so that you receive the most from your first deal, financially with personal growth and you are naturally growing your business or brand.

The biggest problem for my readers and others investing in real estate, is that they will not know what to do with the money after they have closed the deal. It is so much harder to keep the money than to close your first deal! However, I can tell you the way and explain to you the do's and the do nots of real estate. If you follow the 5 laws, you will not have any problems, but, if you are going to divert from this path in any way you will have no one to blame for not winning but yourself. LAW 1 is the money obtained from property sales is not for you to go and buy a luxury vehicle or a fancy home, and the money should not be used for a fancy trip or expensive jewelry either. This money must and will, go back into buying more property and only after you have completed three or four Flips and have secured your properties to collect a steady income of rent, then you can venture off into another business or buy an affordable personal gift you desire as a reward for completing and accomplishing your goals. By this time you should have

———— ◆ ◆ ◆ ————

Law 1
The money obtained from property sales is not for you to go and buy luxuries.

————————————

plishing your goals. By this time you should have a nice security nest. The reason I say, other business or smaller nice thing you desire is because everyone's dream is not just to have real estate and collect rent. You may want to own a franchise of some sort of business outside of real-estate, but that is for you to know and decide. I'm only here to help build your foundation in real-estate, so that you can explore other avenues of business and follow your dreams. I am going to tell you right now, getting your investment capital is your own task. I can help you if you do not have startup capital. This book serves as a great learning and resource tool for you, but without capital you will not make capital as fast. You may have access to cash and not know. Your credit is capital. If you have good credit or a hard money lender that will loan you your money for the investment and believes in your business, that will be your start. You may be able to secure a loan from a family member or a close friend or girlfriend who may believe in your business venture. Now on to another important part of the book, my blueprint on how to win in the field of real estate. My thoughts, and these you must understand, are my thoughts that I have lived by and have had excellent success through the wins and losses of purchasing property. Starting off with your first property, some may vary from a duplex or a single-family home, but it all pans out to the same in the end for all investors that follow the plan, and that is money being made and being able to install a plan that can be repeated over and over to keep cashing a check and growing the business! My first property was a $10,000 duplex, I had to put $16,000 into the property in order to get it in a condition that was considered marketable. Once finished, I then asked my grandmother to check her credit score. After seeing that her score was in the 750 range, I then looked for a local lender that she and I were comfortable with. (You can use your personal bank, Chase, Wells Fargo, or

Bank Of America whatever your bank may be is fine.) I'm simply explained my situation, that I own a property free and clear and I have a buyer that wants the home after seeing the extensive repairs that were done to the property. This lead to me building a great rapport with that individual and learning more about what was needed to secure a loan and sell a home. The lender would have to be able to process the deals that I have structured, in one deal I would forfeit (Gift or Lend) 3% - 5% of the down payment needed to purchase the home into the account of the trustworthy and creditworthy individual, my Grandmother, who will be the purchaser. (If the purchaser already has the money in their account, you will not have to give them this money for the down payment!) Once the money was in her account for thirty days it was seasoned. (Seasoned money is money that has been in a credible bank for 60 to 90 days.) At the time, I listed the property with prudential. I then had my grandmother put in her offer to purchase and I except that offer and we went to closing. At that point my beautiful grandmother, Bernice Breaker, had just, in that act of support, helped her grandson become a first-generation businessman. I closed the deal on that home at 3524 North 15th Street Milwaukee, WI 53206 in 2002 for $69,000.00. Four years later I sold that same home to a good friend of mine for $85,000.00. She now lives there rent free because she collects $750.00 from the upstairs two-bedroom apartment and lives in the lower two-bedroom apartment with her dad, a war veteran who pays her rent $375.00 a month, and that allows her to pay her $675.00 a month mortgage with Wells Fargo Bank much easier. She is now providing a great environment for her dad and saving money while gaining equity in the property. She can look for another home to move into as she collects rent from the duplex and now she can move into a two family that she can live in and collect rent again or buy a single family and live alone. She can use the first property as a rental investment and collect rent monthly. The mortgage on the property is $675.00. If the two apartments are rented for $750.00 a piece, that totals $1500.00. She has a positive income every month of $825.00 before water bills and taxes are calculated. This is call building positive monthly cash flow.

BEFORE & AFTER

◆ ◆ ◆

One of the great lessons in this book is: Know who you are and what you want to achieve in both business and in life! You will develop habits of success by looking at those around that you admire and that are doing well in business and in life. List the reasons you look at the person as a good businessman or woman. Again list the reason you admire them and compare them to someone that is successful in business and in the areas you want to tackle. The person you pick should be above or equally strong as the person you admire. If the per-

◆ ◆ ◆

Know who you are and what you want to achieve in both business and in life!

son is accessible to you, determine if they are as good as you thought, and if so, then move forward from there to positioning yourself for mentorship / mentoring. You ultimately do not need the person to be there to mentor you. Mentoring can be from a distance. You can watch their moves and the things they may accomplish and how they go about accomplishing there goals on line. You may also want to research and see if they have videos or a book written. If possible, ask you mentor or the person you admire for information on how they accomplished their endeavor and explain to them what it is that you want to achieve. Emulate their good business habits to help you on your way to success. If the person that you want information on is successful or a great business woman or man it will be easy to google them and find out as much information as possible that is available online. Remember: It is easy to do research and read up on whoever you admire and respect.

Robert Pyles – After high school, Mr. Pyles went into the US Air Force where he served for 15 years, living in Korea, North Dakota and Cheyenne, Wyoming. It was there that he started working at McDonald's part-time at night and on weekends to make some extra cash. One of his mentors, Don Thompson, suggested he check out some restaurants in Milwaukee, a city Pyles knew little about. Pyles is an Alabama native who opened his first McDonald's in Milwaukee 21 years ago. Today, he operates 13 McDonald's restaurants in Milwaukee. He is the only African-American McDonald's franchise owner in Wisconsin. But there is more. He is also a minister at Abundant Faith Church of Integrity on Good Hope Road in Milwaukee Wisconsin. As if that was not a lot to manage, Mr. Pyles is also a commercial and residential property mogul.

Donald Trump – Donald John Trump is the 45th and current President of the United States who took office January 20, 2017. Previously, he was a real estate mogul, and a former reality TV star. Born in Queens, New York in 1971, Trump became involved in large, profitable building projects in Manhattan. In 1980, he opened the Grand Hyatt New York, which made him the city's best-known developer. In 2004, Trump began starring in the hit NBC reality series *The Apprentice*, which also spawned the offshoot *The Celebrity Apprentice*. Trump turned his attention to politics, and in 2015 he announced his candidacy for president of the United States on the Republican ticket. After winning a majority of the primaries and caucuses, Trump became the official Republican candidate for president on July 19, 2016. That November,

Trump was elected the 45th President of the United States, after defeating Democratic candidate Hillary Clinton

Jay - Z – Rapper Jay-Z was born Shawn Corey Carter on December 4, 1969, in Brooklyn, New York. "He was the last of my four children," Jay-Z's mother, Gloria Carter, later recalled, "the only one who didn't give me any pain when I gave birth to him, and that is how I knew he was a special child." His father, Adnes Reeves, left the family when Jay-Z was only 11 years old. The young rapper was raised by his mother in Brooklyn's drug-infested Marcy Projects. He used rap as an escape, appearing for the first time on *Yo! MTV Raps* in 1989. After selling millions of records with his Roc-a-Fella label, Jay-Z created his own clothing line and founded an entertainment company. He wed popular singer and actress Beyoncé in 2008.

Warren Buffet - Born in Nebraska in 1930, Warren Buffett demonstrated keen business abilities at a young age. He formed Buffett Partnership Ltd. in 1956, and by 1965 he had assumed control of Berkshire Hathaway. Overseeing the growth of a conglomerate with holdings in the media, insurance, energy, and the food and beverage industries, Buffett became one of the world's richest men and a celebrated philanthropist.

"Known as the "Oracle of Omaha," Warren Buffett is an investment guru and one of the richest and most respected businessmen in the world."

Steve Forbes - Steve Forbes was born on July 18, 1947, in Morristown, New Jersey. In 1973, he began writing his own column for his father's magazine, *Forbes*. When his father died in 1990, Steve Forbes took over the magazine. In 1993, he founded Empower America. Forbes sought the Republican presidential nomination in 1996 and 2000 but dropped out both times. He became a Freedom Works board member in 2006.

John Willard Marriott - John Willard Marriott was born on September 17, 1900, in Marriott Settlement, Utah. In 1927, he opened an A&W root beer shop in Washington, D.C. and then launched the Hot Shoppe eateries. Marriott eventually became head of the National Restaurant Association and opened the first of the Marriott hotels in 1959.

The chain became one of America's largest companies and developed into an international business.

Steve Jobs – Steven Paul Jobs was an American inventor, designer and entrepreneur who was the co-founder, chief executive and chairman of Apple Computer. Apple's revolutionary products, which include the iPod, iPhone and iPad, are now seen as dictating the evolution of modern technology. Born in 1955 to two University of Wisconsin graduate students who gave him up for adoption. Jobs was smart but without direction, dropped out of college and experimented with different pursuits before co-founding Apple with Steve Wozniak in 1976. Jobs left the company in 1985, launching Pixar Animation Studios, then returned to Apple more than a decade later. Jobs died in 2011 following a long battle with pancreatic cancer.

Bill Gates - William Henry Gates III is an American business magnate, investor, author, philanthropist, humanitarian, and principal founder of Microsoft Corporation Entrepreneur. Bill Gates (born October 28, 1955) and his partner Paul Allen founded and built the world's largest software business, Microsoft, through technological innovation, keen business strategy, and aggressive business tactics. In the process, Gates became one of the richest men in the world.

50 Cent / Curtis Jackson - Curtis James Jackson III, known professionally as 50 Cent, is an American rapper, singer, songwriter, actor, television producer, businessman, and investor. Born in the South Jamaica neighborhood of the borough of Queens, Jackson began selling drugs at age twelve, during the 1980s crack epidemic, but turned his life around to become a entrepreneur and businessman.

Bob Johnson - Robert L. Johnson was born on April 8, 1946, in Hickory, Mississippi. Johnson founded Black Entertainment Television (BET) in 1979 with his wife, Sheila. He became the first African-American billionaire after selling the network to Viacom in 2001. Johnson has since started a new business, the RLJ Companies, and has invested in an NBA team, a film company, and political causes and campaigns. Black Entertainment Television was the first black owned cable network targeting the African-American market. It was launched in January 1980, initially broadcasting for two hours a week. In 1991, <u>BET became the first African American-owned company to be listed on the New York Stock Exchange</u>. The network has continued to grow since that time, reaching tens of millions of homes and expanding to include other traditional and digital channels.

ABOVE AND BEYOND THE CALL OF DUTY

This to me is one of the most important traits in a businessman, businesswoman or a entrepreneur. You have to be willing to go that extra mile; do that late job stay when everyone else wants to leave, you do more than everyone else so that you deserve more than everyone else. Outwork them! You have to do more in order to expect more from life and the universe. Some people are under the impression that you have to work physically hard to attain wealth. I am sorry to say; you are sadly mistaken, It does not have to always be labor or physically hard work it can be time consuming or mentally draining. The work you do does not always have to be physical labor. Doing more does not always mean you have to be at the your office or the property your renovating. You may have to do field work, such as passing out flyers, when the competition does not. Because they do not see the value in passing out flyers. They may not promote their business the way we do. You have to always remember that in order to stay on top, you still have to do more in your business so that it separates you and your company from everyone else. Opposition and competition are two things in the business world that will never change. <u>Competitors</u> are the people with the knowledge to challenge your company. Rich Real Estate will be the cement and steel for your solid foundation in the business your building. Do more to get more, do less and expect less. Whenever you think of quitting, remember all of the times you just stuck in there and finished or succeeded. It is never as bad as you may think it is in the beginning. You have to be personally motivated and want more than everyone else around you. Even when you are tired and everyone else leaves and goes home; you are still working; and to you, even if it is hard work, it is what you love so it is never a problem. When everyone else wants to quit, you still have the motivation to keep going because you have come to know that in order to get more in life, you do more to deserve that special gift; whether it is a time off for vacation, or for your company to double or triple in size because of your dedication. You and your business partners will reap the benefits of your hard work by an improvement of life and living, It allows your children, their children and your close family members to live a better life than what their parents did. On the other hand that does not mean your children will follow in your foot steps to keep the family business going in the future. You have to find the correct person rather son or daughter cousin or friend someone has to love the business as much as you did in order for it to keep growing. I ultimately want it to be a family member that keeps my business going so that generational wealth will be created, and my family's legacy and business will flourish for years to come.

Real-estate fact, first time home buyer may receive a FHA government loans for three percent down payment OF THE SELLING PRICE to purchase the home, $3000.00 down on a $100,000.00 home $9000 down on a $300,000 home.

PERSISTENCE

◆ ◆ ◆

Persistence to me is to chase after your dreams with relentless effort and to follow your first mind by any means necessary, without hurting anyone or yourself. There is no fun in being wealthy in jail or with health problems. So, while remaining persistent, take care of yourself and be mindful of the people you deal with and the bridges you build and burn. During your business trials and obstacles, "which is throughout the life of you being in business", you will meet people that will not agree with your plans or dreams. Stay persistent in what you believe in and do not get side tracked because of what others think. Constructive criticism is sometimes cool and at other times cruel, so remain focused, and as bad as it may sound, never let a person with less than what you have dictate how you go about building your foundation, and do not ask their opinion on your business either. Remember "constructive criticism" can be more destructive than anyone intended. If people have not seen the things you have seen or been where you have been, they can not exactly understand the message your trying to get across to them on building your business, sometimes. Know that what you may be talking about can and may sound foreign to them, do not feel bad if they say your plans are crazy. Do your research on the business you are pursuing so that you know the true ups and downs of that business. Proper preparation prevents poor performance in any situation, God willing. If you can find a business that you like to get involved in that makes money, and you can repeat it in other locations or with other people, I think you may have found something to be persistent about! I say that because you have to like, live, and love the business that your persistence is dedicated to. Without the persistence and dedication, your chances of failing are severe. Who wants to try hard at something they really do not like or want to do? You may fall down a few times in the real estate investment business so you have to love your business and want to win really bad in order to keep getting up to fight for that business to win. Unless your very lucky and happen to hit the lottery or find that there is oil on your investment property. Like everything, history repeats itself, so if you know the business you like, love, and are ready to live, then do the research. Find out the things the millionaire or billionaire in your business field did in order to get as big as they are and follow their lead with persistence and perseverance towards your goal and win. Real estate allows you the options of building a trust field with tangible securities that others can see and understand that profit and progress is being made in our area. A strong leader builds an even stronger team of people who are persistent even when he may not want to be (**the team not knowing that**), because even the person with the most persistence can not always do it all alone! Life gives you the support you will need if you ask for it. Meaning there are people who are in the same field as you and would love to support what you are doing and get paid. You just have to look for your supporting cast of people that believe in you and your dreams and all of a sudden with work and persistence your dreams aligned in some way. Sometimes it may take a few minutes to get your rehab / property repair crew together but once you organized your repair crew. Money will be saved as you build and grow your business and company. People are people, some who may or may not have as much as you, or some who may have more than you. The people you want around are the ones that want you to win as much as they want to win themselves. People that will support you and champion you forward to greatness are the people that you want and need around. Do not become complacent in your business dealings and everyday work. Instead consider the fact that

The people you want around are the ones that want you to win as much as they want to win themselves.

you have a strong team that supports you and that allows you to take on the major work and delegate everything else accordingly throughout the TEAM. The foundation you have laid and shown your team and people can really work is what can makes your business grow and helps others to grow their business and be successful. What people may have thought to be luck, or a rare occurrence is actually attainable, and they can be involved in that situation or the dream to be a part of the upper class in society by being persistent. You have to remain captain of the ship even when there is rough sailing knowing you will make it through is conditioning that will help others to believe and know how to stay strong in the time property ups and downs.

LAW 2 The way to remain in a good space in the real estate market is to always buy more property every time you sell a property this is one of my business Laws. Buy fix and rent, the more property you obtain the more income you have coming in. One of the best practices in buying property, is buying multi-units as fast as possible. Once you have the knowledge of rehab repair under you belt. The multi-units allows you to have multiple apartments but only one location to pay taxes on, oppose to having six duplex (Six two Family Homes) properties that would be a total of twelve apartments, but the six properties are six property taxes that have to be paid. A low cost twelve unit building, or two six-unit building would save you money and allow you to collect rent in one to two locations. Always remember (BFR) BUY FIX and RENT as soon as possible weather it is a multi-unit or a single family property get it done and get it rented. If you ever

---

Law 2
Buy more property every time you sell a property.

---

get tired just remember there are people all over the world that would lose days of sleep and food to have the opportunities we have to buy and sell these properties for a great profit. The flip side of BFR is BFS **BUY FLIP SELL**. You do not have to hold on to every property you buy, and you do not have to sell everything, It is to your discretion once you get to that point.

KNOWLEDGE

◆ ◆ ◆

The knowledge that I am referring to is basically reading books to gain relevant information in the area that you are trying to succeed and win in. Malcolm X once said, "If you want to hide something from a black man, put it in a book." Ever since I heard that said, I have found it hard to separate myself from reading different books and researching more knowledge in my field of business, real estate investing. All the knowledge you need is in every library around the world. I am sure what you are looking for will be online. The internet is your best friend for knowledge and information. Most of the time what we are searching for is not even that far from where we are working or standing at the moment we are looking for it. Information is everywhere around us. We just have to know what it is we are looking for and how to properly utilize the information correctly. The internet has a vast array of different avenues and websites. As far as obtaining knowledge of real estate or real estate business goes, you can choose and pick what you want to read or listen to. You can look for your first property on the internet without having a physical real estate agent. You can get the ball rolling on your plans without even dealing with a realtor yet. It is very important you use this tool to your advantage just so you know what you are looking for and what is out there, before someone else tells you what you are looking for and what is out there. You have to understand I have made this process of buying and selling real estate cut and dry for my readers. Some of the books you may have read are written for the pleasure of reading and not really the subject matter it supposed to be about. Some books may have a good title, but that does not necessarily mean that it will holster good information. You should research the author to see if they have made any accomplishments in the field that they are writing their books about. There are many people who feel as though they are qualified to write a book solely because of some major research they have done in the field, however never actually physically putting themselves in those situations to truly succeed in that field. You should know the history of the author of the books you are reading because their perspectives are going to influence your way of thinking and doing business. It would not make sense to follow the likes of someone, not knowing who they are or what they are about. Do your research on everything from beginning to end, that way nothing should be above your understanding. For instance, you may not want to do your electrical work yourself, but knowledge as simple as knowing that a ground and a positive does not go together, could help you. Just knowing a good electricians number may be a better help, LOL. One of the best practices is to explore what worked best for the home owners that sold property in your area that are similar to your home. I know that a popular method for the Midwest is to have your realtor or lawyer "comp", meaning check comparable homes of similar size, condition, age and style in the area or neighborhood. Compare the property that you are looking to purchase with the similar properties that have sold in the area for an exceptional price, so then you can set the sale price for the home you are going to list to be sold. Now get to work closing on your property and repairing it so you can make a profit and buy more homes to make more money. It is the American way! Buy Flip

Sell, Buy Flip Rent BFS, BFR.

REFINANCE

◆ ◆ ◆

Another way to receive money out of a property you own is to refinance the money out of the location. This may only be an option to people with good credit or the credit needed to secure the loan against the property. Yes it is a loan that your taking against you property. The owner of the property also has to have enough equity in the property that they are trying to refinance. Equity is the amount of money or the cash value that is maintained in the home. The longer you own a property mortgage the longer you pay your mortgage the more equity you will gain in the property. You will have full equity in the home or property if it is fully paid for, meaning free and clearly owned, no debt remaining. This gives you the option to refinance a rental property that you collect rent from monthly and own free and clear or a property that you do not own free and clear but the positive income you receive from the property allows you to make the mortgage payment and at the same time save and make the necessary repairs to the property when they needed. The tenants will pay the monthly mortgage that is placed on the property to secure the loan or in other words to secure the amount of money you have borrowed from the bank. This will allow you to still retain ownership of the property and get cash on hand to buy more property. I am a firm believer in going to where you bank at to get your first refinance quote be very careful not to allow anyone to pull your credit while searching for the best rate. If your credit is pulled an inquiry may lower your score and may jeopardize your chances of refinancing the property and you do not want that. Your credit score is what will determine how much your interest rate will be on the loan, the higher you score the better your interest rate supposedly. You want to refinance with a company that will allow your loan to have a no penalty early pay off option. Some loan companies have a penalty that you may be subjected to if you pay off your loan earlier than the date that the loan was dated to be paid off, the reason being is they will not be able to collect the amount of interest if the life of the loan is shorter than expected. It is in your best regards to pay extra every month on your loan to cut the interest your paying . The reason I suggest that you pay extra money on your loan every month is because initially the majority of the payment you make in the beginning will be going directly towards the interest. You will not be making a noticeable dent in your principal at all. (The principal being the original amount of money you borrowed from the bank or lender without the interest attached.) So the less principal you have the less interest you will be paying on the money that you borrowed. You want the extra money that you are paying to go directly to the principal. When you send in your mortgage payment include a letter saying the extra amount that you are paying and you want it put directly towards the principal. In some instances the original bank or lender that gave you the loan will sell your loan to another company. So the name and location that you where once sending your payments may change unexpectedly. That does not mean you should not send in your mortgage payment. A letter should accompany the new payment or should come before the payment letting you know that your loan has been purchased buy another bank or company.

RUSH FIX

◆ ◆ ◆

My example of a rush fix is basically buying a low-cost property in a low to mid-range priced area and you as the property owner, make the bare minimum of repairs (carpet and flooring, light fixtures, plugs, light switches, painting all the walls, and the ceilings white, fixing broken windows, new entry doors, exterior lighting, the bathrooms vanity an fixtures). Make sure you change the kitchens water fixture and maybe the cabinets if you and your contractor feel the need. These are all things that should be done in order to successfully complete a rush fix. You put money into this property and its renovations are done now. You are ready to see a profit from the fix and sale without doing top dollar repairs. Keep in mind that knowing the home is just as important as knowing the area. A home in a bad area may be a low repair cost initially, but it may not sell for what you think it should be worth, or even worse, it might take longer than you planned and you may have to pay back a loan or debt. Always be prepared for the unforeseen circumstances. Most neighborhoods with a low police presence, drug activity, robbery, car theft and other violent situations are all red flags. Sometimes you may want to buy that property in that area as a rental property as a good deal, but not just starting out unless you are building your rental property to produce you positive income. That property for a small price may be a big problem because of the area it is in. Just remember the location you buy your property in can make your repair easy or hard. You do not want to start doing repairs and people breaking in to steal your new fixtures or heating systems because of the area and you not knowing the area. **LAW 3** This is how to find the best areas and homes to buy for a rush fix and flip. You should always check and see what the homes are selling for in the area where you are planning on purchasing your property first. Me, personally, I do. I like to check the housing market to see what homes nearby are currently selling for

Law 3
Always check the
"comps" first.

and what they have sold for. I also like to set up a walk through of local properties that are for sale to see the repairs the other guy has done. This way, if the property you are looking to purchase is similar to any one of the homes that have sold in the area for a good price then you are making a good buy. At this point you will have a somewhat good estimate on how much you may sell your property for. If you buy a cheap property in a low-cost area, you may not be able to get the property to appraise at a price high enough for you to make a substantial profit after the sale. So, take heed that this is very serious. Be sure to do your homework on what the property you are buying can sell for. It is also very important that you have a team that works and believes in you, your vision and dream, so that they do not think it is just all about you. No, it is your vision. There is no I in the word TEAM. Finding a good team that works for a great price is one of the most important aspect of repairing a rush fix or any rehab project, your repair crew. If the labor is too expensive, your profit decreases which could make flipping the home less profitable for you. Know your costs, know your workers, and know your business. My grandmother Bernice Breaker Williams, always told me **"Let the people run their mouths Daryl while you keep running your business" -"Bernice**

Breaker Williams". That has been the best advice of my life. I always listen to the gifts of knowledge she gives to me my grandma at 87 years old. Next thing to always remember starting out is to write down every dollar you spend that has to do with the property. Save all your receipts to file taxes and to add up your repair and materials. Secure a book to write down things that need to be done on an everyday basis. At the end of every work day you should write down the money you paid for all labor, from cutting the grass to installing your furnace and hot water heater, every dollar spent should be accounted for. You want to be sure that you are not only saying you are making money on the home you flip, but you are understanding and knowing how much and why you made money off of this property you have flipped. Every cost cut saves you money, but the best way to save on any project is to save money on labor and material both. To save money on labor, you will need to tap into the locals in the area that the neighbors may use for an electrical problem. He or

> *"Let the people run their mouths while you keep running your business."*
> *-"Bernice Breaker Williams"*

she may be more or less skilled. You have to give it a shot but know that they have done the kind of work your looking for in the past. Whoever can do the job 100% and save you time and money that is the person who you should choose. The easiest way for you to see if they can do the job is to ask to see their last job or to do a walkthrough of the last big job they completed. If their last job was a year ago, that person may not be the one you want to entrust in doing your rehab job. Home Depot, Menards, Lowe's or any home repair store is a great location to meet a contractor. I say, look for the one in the parking lot with a good van not the best van just good, and his or her company name on the side with a phone number. Get as many numbers as possible from different contractors that can offer you different skills for different jobs you need done to complete your property. Start calling and getting estimates as soon as possible. Never pay for an estimate. A good contractor will do it for free. Try not to schedule the meeting at the same time so that the contractors do not try to come to-gether on a lock in price on you. They may know each other. Do not take the chance. Always listen to what they say they will do within their repairs and write down everything they say they will do. Your next move is to get the contractor to give you an invoice from their company showing all of the repairs that will be done on this property. A professional contractor will have a contractor's license in the city or state that you are located; and they should always have contractor's insurance or company insurance. You can not sue or get any money from the contractor right away if they are not insured. You will have to sue them in court and waste a lot of time. Your project will be on hold and you are out of the money you paid the person to do the work until the case is over. Never give money to a contractor you do not know before work begins! Tell the contractor you will be buying all the material and keeping it with you until the work begins. Once you build a good report with your contractor and you know where he lives, LOL. Then you can have him or her get the material for the job you are doing while you continue on looking for other potential investments to flip or keep to rent out.

IMAGINATION

---◆◆◆---

"Imagination is better than knowledge"

– Albert Einstein

A thought formed solely from what you have seen or know from your thinking as a child and your imagination is what helps you find new ways to play or enjoy yourself, whether you are with other children or alone. What you truly imagine in your wildest dreams can be achieved if you use what you imagine to motivate you to get what you want to have or accomplish in life. Think and grow, meaning if you want to buy a duplex rental property, you have to take the inspiration that you have or the image from your imagination find a photo of a property that is similar to the one you want and then read and keep reading anything that has a similar comparison to what you are doing or trying to attain read about how to buy a property where the lowest properties are, who the easiest sellers are. You want to acquire knowledge before you jump in and go buy a property. You can complete what it is you are trying to accomplish easier by reading and learning the business you are in. If you are not worrying about ever helping someone else or ever losing what you have then there is no need to know how to get back up. Once you have lost something, in order to get it back, you have to know how you got it in the first place. To know where you are going you have to understand and know where you come from and where you want to be. Remember and understand, for the time it takes to attain wealth, it can all be lost in a matter of seconds even if it took years to attain. So, I am saying you should do all your homework on whatever it is that you are investing in or buying, be it a car, stocks, property, or a company. Do the back-ground check on whatever it is you decide. Try to never make a decision from emotions. Never decide in business with feelings. Think it through. Use knowledge and understanding of the situation at hand. If the emotions are because the person you are going to do business with is an ass

Never make a decision from emotions.

and it will cause more problems in the long run or the deal has a structural problem, then step away, put an end to the deal. That is just a good move and a smart decision to make as a boss. Know when to walk away and when to stick it out. That decision is very important throughout business and in life. Picking the wars to fight and the ones to evade. That is what you take from your life's experiences, good and bad. Learn from experiences; realize what brings you joy and gives you strength, and what drains your power and takes your happiness away. The key is to identify those things. Keep the bad ones as far away from you as possible, and keep the good ones close so that you are always in a positive space, even when things seem to be bad. Your thoughts are more powerful than you can imagine. If you knew how important your good vibes and thoughts were you would protect your happiness by any means necessary.

REALITY

Reality is the acceptance of what is true; the state of being true. Knowing your limitations right now in life and using that as a strength is the best reality for an investor. Knowing that it will take you one to three years to get an electrical license, so you hire an electrician; that is knowing your limitations. The same goes with plumbing and so on unless that is a skill you want to learn for your personal preference. Doing a big electrical job is not in your skill set, you do the next best thing and hire a professional to do the job. You understand that some things are out of your limitations. In today's society, in certain cities and states it is just a reality for the average Joe or an entrepreneur to just purchase a property at a low price, fix it and it is worth jumps fifty percent or double the amount it was originally

> *Knowing your limitations right now in life and using that as a strength is the best reality for an investor.*

purchased for if not more. You have to know what properties in the area are selling for to really understand and know what your profit will be when you sell the property. You have to understand that the property you are selling should be the same or similar to the ones you are looking at in the area. So that you know what your property could possibly sell for realistically. One of my courses of action is to always check the foundation on a property before anything else. I myself stay away from a property that has major foundation problems. If the home is in an excellent area and has serious foundation problems, all bets are off on that purchase. I realize my limitations and I know my real estate comfortable area. You may say at this point, "What the hell is a real estate comfortable area?", because no one is really ever comfortable in real estate before they are financially stable. Do not include people or investors that have other streams of income from different business ventures. A comfortable area is when you have enough money coming in from your rental properties to cover the worst repairs a tenant could do in a location or a natural problem that needed to be repaired in one of your properties. That income allows you to save, purchase, repair, and sell other properties. This is building your income and your real estate portfolio.

F.E.A.R.
False Evidence Appearing to be Real

———————◆◆◆———————

Fear of failing and not being able to get back up. The fear of not getting back what you put out. The fear of no one knowing your win or accomplishments. The fear of dying before you complete your dreams. I think these are all respectable things to fear but not to the point that it will not allow you to take a risk at financial freedom in real estate or in business. I feel that as long as you try to do good you should receive good in life and in business. That does not mean be a push over and let people take advantage of you. Be humble. Stay business and growth minded. Remember if it sounds too good to be true, it usually is, unless you have done proper research, then it is a come up. We always have to pray that God and the universe will not give us more than we can handle. If it seems like He has, then we ask he gives us knowledge and strength to keep trying and to learn from our mistakes and keep pushing on to win. If you believe that there is something bigger than yourself, I believe you can pull through. No one is perfect in life and we all make mistakes. An act done over and over is not a mistake. A mistake is a person wronging you or you wronging another person. A lot of times in life what goes around comes around and the act of wrong was not worth it. Try and stay positive. Life is about decisions and options. Before you choose not to do something because of fear, stop and ask yourself, "what would happen if I was not scared and I pushed on?" It is all about the knowledge do your research to move forward you should not be afraid of what you understand! Believe what your about to do is what your meant to do, it is your life's plan. Mentally that is where you should be with your goal. Being scared and fearful is usually an emotion due to the lack of knowledge and understanding of the particular situation. A part of fear is knowing you can not control everything in life, nor make everything go your way always. Believe in you and love yourself in order to step inside of the business world and outside of your home or comfort space! You should cut back on your spending and purchasing things that are not assets. For you to grow your money, it has to be saved and reinvested. If real estate is the machine that made you money, that is what you should be repeating: purchasing more properties to grow your business. When you buy that property, you are investing in yourself. You are saying that you believe in yourself enough to push forward and not be the norm, to not fear what people may say is a bad market, real estate, or good buy. Believe in yourself, what you see, know, read, and have done and lived through. Remember thing that you have learned from your mentors and what the Laws are in this book. Do what you can do because what everyone else may be doing might not be good for you. Never question what you know to be true. Someone else may try and put a doubt in your mind by saying something that is not the same as what you have done or may be thinking about doing. You may have achieved or attained things that others may not have or they may not have been fortunate enough to see the things you have seen in business and in life. Their lower level of investing knowledge or business knowledge leads them to believe that what you are

When you buy that property, you are investing in yourself.

saying can not work and will not be possible. Never ask the advice of others with less than you. If it did not work for them it probably won't work for you is their mindset! They place their failure in business or fears of failing on you. Knowing yourself and what you are capable of and what you can endure and accomplish will allow you to go further in life than people who are still trying to find themselves and who question their own strengths. I have found that the biggest learning experience in life is failing. Failing allows you to find an inner security, an inner strength to keep pushing on. If you fall you get up and do not lay there. That fall teaches you things you could not learn any other way. Failure allows you to discover your strong will to win and your strength not to give up. Failure allows you to find your inner discipline. "Know that by reading this book, it shows your will to win and be different." You have to be disciplined to not give up; to get back in motion when things slow down or the project does not go right; to change and or eliminate the things that may have hindered your success in the past. Failure erases FEAR in that particular space you are in because you come out of that failed situation with the knowledge and a lesson on what not to do again! Failure also allows you to know and understand who are in your INNER CIRCLE and who your TRUE FRIENDS ARE. "A TRUE FRIEND WILL SHINE DURING TRYING TIMES." You do not truly know yourself or the strength of your inner circle or friends until both have been tested by unforeseen circumstances and adversities. To know who is really with you is truly a great blessing in life and in business, but always be aware that things and people also change with time. You do not want to FEAR calling on a friend when you are in need. You may need to borrow $10,000 - $50,000 to close a $150,000 deal. You do not want to get to the end of a deal and need money to close and can not call on anyone! You should ultimately have your own money as a person in the business world doing real estate deals, but there may be a time you may have gotten in over your head or it is a great deal that you can not lose in! This is the time when the **thought** of it is not always *what* you know but *who* you know should kick in. I have found that the best people to have in your inner circle are people that are like minded but slightly diversified, in business and in life. What happens is, you may want the same things out of life or have the same goals as the people in your circle, but everyone plays a different part in completing the project. You may not have a degree in law but someone in your circle may have a degree, you may not have a real estate license which will allow you more options in purchasing property but a person in your inner circle does, and so on electrical, plumbing and heating may be all trades of people in your inner circle or friends of people in your inner circle. In business, 40% is about *what* you know and 60% is about *who* you know. Things can be easier if the people you deal with are good people. You want to attract people who do the work you need done on an everyday basis! Remember alone you are 1 but with a TEAM,

> *In business, 40% is about what you know and 60% is about who you know.*

friends, comrades or business associates you can be many. You do not have a business until it runs successfully while you are not there. If you have to be there to run your business every day, you do not have a business, you still have a Job! You have a truly successful business when you can leave, and people want that business to win as much or more than you do its their bread and butter also, so they make sure it continues to produce. Hire people who need you as much or more than you need them. The appreciation after the win together is much better. They understand that they earned their position and you wanted them in that position. You grow and help them grow at the same time. Owners earn, make and take their positions in life, a partner helps the dream grow, workers are given a position to make an owner or partner more! A worker is no longer a worker when he understands why. The person who knows why will always be the boss of the person who knows how until the person who knows how understand why. What I am saying is yes have a skill, electrician, plumber, carpenter, and so on, be great at that skill and utilize that skill to become an investor and buy a property. Relationships you have built with other contractors should come into play when it is time to repair the investment you have purchased. Give a couple of friends and contractors you know that have home repair skills a call and start getting prices for your repairs. Do not be worried if you do not know everyone some of your friends that you have done jobs for may have a few contractors you can utilize for your first property rehab. Always try and maintain balance with the things you want so they do not become more important than the means and the way you obtain those things!

Places and things to know as a entrepreneur

---◆◆◆---

CHAMBER OF COMMERCE - Any Chambers of Commerce in the city your business is located or where you do business at is an excellent source of information.

CITY HALL - A city hall or town hall is the headquarters of a city or towns administration and usually houses the city or town council, its associated department, and their employees. It is also usually the base of the city, town, borough or county mayor.

VISTA PRINT: For your print needs: business cards, flyers, brochures, letter heads, and a lot more office and business and promotional products.

GOTPRINT: A company for your print needs business cards, flyers, brochures, letter heads, and more office, business and promotional products

Dunn & Bradstreet - Dun & Bradstreet is a corporation that offers information on commercial credit as well as reports on businesses. Most notably, Dun & Bradstreet is recognizable for its Data Universal Numbering System (DUNS numbers); these generate business information reports for more than 100 million companies around the globe.

Yelp – Yelp is the king of reviews. It may not be structured like every other social networking sites but Yelp has more than 140 million active users.

Mogul - Mogul is an all-inclusive technology platform and mobile app that enables women worldwide to connect, converse, and access knowledge from each other. It was founded in 2014 by Tiffany Pham and David Pham.

TripAdvisor - TripAdvisor, Inc. is an American travel and restaurant website company that shows hotel and restaurant reviews, accommodation bookings and other travel-related content. It also includes interactive travel forums. TripAdvisor was an early adopter of user-generated content.

FaceBook – I feel this is one of the most popular social media website, boasting more than 1.5 billion active monthly users. This platform is particularly great for small business that are looking to show your businesses or your products or events.

FourSquare - Foursquare is a location "check-in" service that allows your customers to tell the world that they are in your place of business. They can as well share this info with their friends. Like Yelp, this is a must use platform for all small local businesses.

LinkedIn - Consider this as your online resume. You can list your business history, core objectives and skill as well as a recommendation from customers. A sound LinkedIn profile might see you win incredible business offers.

Twitter - Twitter's value lies in its ability for your posts to go viral. You can use the platform to post your business updates, recent news and more.

Myspace - Myspace is a social networking website offering an interactive, user-submitted network of friends, personal profiles, blogs, groups, photos, music, and videos.

Craigslist - Craigslist is an American classified advertisements website with sections devoted to jobs, housing, for sale, items wanted, services, community, gigs, resumés, and discussion forums. Craig Newmark began the service in 1995 as an email distribution list to friends, featuring local events in the San Francisco Bay Area.

Pinterest - People use Pinterest to discover and save ideas. Ideas can take lots of forms, from recipes to renovation projects to the perfect pair of shoes.

Snapchat – Snapchat is an image processing application that has quickly grown in popularity.

AngelList – If your trying to raise some extra funds for your startup, I feel you need to try out AngleList, a social network that connects startups with investors.

Instagram – This Web-site / app allows you to eliminate clutter, highlighting your products and services in a very original way. I feel it works best with products, you can still use the website to show business accomplishments such as involvement in charity, travel, parties, short video and pictures.

Tumblr – Working the site can prove to be a bit confusing for first timers, Tumblr is a truly inter-esting tool that allows you to post videos, photos, chats, audio messages and quotes. You can also blog / repost your favorite posts.

Youtube – Besides being the second largest search engine, this site is also owned by Google so when it comes to search engine optimization, their videos are more likely to be on Google's top search results. It can also be used as a feedback platform.

Affluence – I feel that all accomplished businessmen and woman looking to connect with other industry experts, should utilize Affluence. This is more of a private social network where industry experts connect, share information and engage in relevant conversations.

Quora - This question and answer platform allows you to set yourself as an expert in your field. Offer consistent, credible answers and see traffic to your website increase.

Google My Business - Google My Business is a free and easy-to-use tool for businesses and organizations to manage their online presence across Google, including Search and Maps. By verifying and editing your business information, you can both help customers find you and tell them the story of your business.

- Manage how your business information appears across Google, including Search and Maps, using Google My Business—for free.

- Interact with customers new and old and tell them the story of your business.
- Get started at google.com/business.

10

Ask yourself what is it that you want out of your real estate business. What are the goals you are setting or the accomplishments you want to make in real estate. I have put 10 questions together to help guide you in your real estate business. If you stick to your goals you will win.

(1) Do you want to buy all you properties in the same area or state?

(2) Who will you have repair your first project?

(3) What type of property will you buy?
   A single family = one family home?
   A duplex home = two family home?
   A multifamily = two+ units in one building?
   A business or commercial property?

(4) Will you finance your property or buy it cash so there are no mortgage payments?

(5) What will be the first thing you repair and or replace in your new property?

(6) Have you started your investment company legally, with your Tax ID #, LLC, INC or some form of corporate filling with your state and the IRS?

(7) What will get you through the repair process when you may be burned out and feel you can not keep going?

(8) Have you been around a person that flips property and completes the home repairs similar or the same as how you would like to?

(9) Do you know the bare minimum of home repair and how things are done? Drywall, plumbing, electrical, heating, exterior repairs, the roof the gutters, cement, and the windows?

(10) Do you have the income capital or financing to completely finish the project ahead of you with or without the unforeseen circumstances?

The 3 L's of Life

◆ ◆ ◆

LISTEN: (Webster Dictionary) *To pay attention to sound to hear something with thoughtful attention and or give consideration. To be alerting to catch an expected sound.*

I realized how important these 3 words are while on a field trip to the local zoo with my 10 - year-old son Karon and his classmates. I was the chaperon of five young kings from my son's class. As we proceeded through the winter weather on the outdoor and indoor zoo trip the young men began to run in different direction wanting to see different thing at the same time. This is when it hit me to explain to the young kings that if they listened, we could not only see everything but learn about the things we were seeing as a group. I explained that they would learn and be able to lead their younger brothers and sisters or their class mates if they can first lead themselves.

LEARN: (Webster Dictionary) *To gain knowledge or understanding of a skill by study, instruction or experience.*

LEAD: (Webster Dictionary) *To direct the operations, activity, or performance of, to have charge of. To guide on a way especially by going in advance, to direct on a course or in a direction.*

Property Repair Checklist

Address _____ Yr Built _____ Br/Ba _____ SqFt _____

- **Roof** (curled, wavy) $ _____
- **Yard** (gutters? dead trees? junk cars? fence? landscaping, extra lot? dimensions?) $ _____
- **Driveway** (exist? broken? shared w/neighbor [easement]?) $ _____
- **Deck / Porch** (add: dimensions/ repair) ? $ _____
- **Gutters** (holes, missing drain pipes, non-existent) $ _____
- **Structural** (rotten/sagging/missing beams, piers, sill plate?) $ _____
- **Crawl/Bsmt wet** (seep thru found., re-slope yard/soil, leaky plumbing/HWH, furn drain line)? $ _____
- **Heat & A/C** (furnace/compressor condition? exist? if no, electrical?) $ _____
- **Plumbing** (galvanized/gray steel or white PVC) ? $ _____
- **Electrical** (2-prong outlets? fuses/circ breakers? amps? skinny/thick main line?) $ _____
- **Paint** exterior (brick?) & interior $ _____
- **Paint** Interior $ _____
- **Demolition** (describe and guestimate qty of dumpsters and demo labor $10/hr) $ _____
- **Flooring** (wobbly/weak :structural; water/urine stains, carpet over bad hdwds? % replacing) $ _____
- **Drywall** (qty of new walls/ceil, wall/ceil patch) ? Insulation? $ _____
- **Carpentry Trim** (stairs? new ceil moudling, baseboards, doors/window mould) ? $ _____
- **Kitchen** (repair/replace cabs? appliances? sinks) ? $ _____
- **Bathrooms** (repair/replace cabs? toilet? bath/sinks) ? $ _____
- **Lighting Fixtures** (lights, ceiling fans, security lights, smoke alarms) ? $ _____
- **Plumbing Fixtures** (faucets, shower heads, sinks) $ _____
- **Windows / Doors** (qty to replace/repair?) $ _____
- **Insulation** (Check if addt'l required in attic) $ _____
- **Addition** (size? remember to use addtl. after-addition, total sq footage in above formulas) $ _____
- **Alarm** $ _____
- **Cleaning & Hauling** $ _____
- **Staging** $ _____

Grand Total $ _____

_____   _____
SIGNATURE   DATE

68

BUSINESS OVER BULLSHIT, ALWAYS.

INTENTIONS

You can not hide from yourself. You have to make your mind up about what you intend on accomplishing so that you know when you are close to achieving your goal. Set a goal and intend on surpassing that goal. Look past that goal to what is next after you have completed the goal you set. Life is about what you truly feel from your heart and what you intend on accomplishing and doing. You will not get the reward of truly accomplishing the goal if you do not complete the task, but with every unsuccessful attempt and short coming there is something to be learned if you push forward and want to win in whatever it is your doing. Life will reward you with knowledge, and the gift of your struggle will be hands on learning. That can not be taught. Knowing your business will give you the option to explain to someone else how to grow or start in real estate investing you never know who is watching your growth from a distance and may want to support your efforts to move forward or win. Be great in what your passion is. You know what your thing is because it will feel right and it gives you the power to go on every day. You may be tired and want to sleep lying in bed. But if a call comes in that furthers your dream or mission you hop up without hesitation and get to where you need to be to do whatever it is that has to be done. Life will always test you with trials and situations. You have to know that whatever your dealing with is just what it is. Face it head on and move forward, the longer you try to avoid the action that has to be addressed the longer the problem will continue to be just that, a problem. A problem is no longer a problem once you address it. Once addressed it becomes a situation dealt with, good or bad its confronted. You now can move on to correct the problem or repay the debt owed on a broken window, crashed car, or settle an old business misunderstanding. If you intend to do good you will do good and get the benefits of the good you have done

A problem is no longer a problem once you address it. It becomes a situation dealt with.

because you know you deserve it. Make a way for someone and God and the universe will make a way for you, small or big.

 A useful or valuable thing, person, or quality

ASSETS

LIABILITIES

 The state of being responsible, especially a debt or financial obligations, debts, arrear, dues.

SHORT SALE, QUICK CLAIM, OR DEED

───────◆─◆─◆───────

By purchasing property's that are in a dis-
tressed condition and not rented or owned by the
city or have an absent landlord, you improve the
look of the area that the property is in and it helps
provide an income for the city that you are buying your property in. When you are paying your
property taxes, pulling repair permits, and paying
your water bill it helps the city's infrastructure. After you purchase a property, the city taxes have to
be paid; which is the strength of all cities that collect property taxes. Collecting taxes from property
owners, both commercial and residential allows
the city to do repairs and improve on things. As
commercial and residential property value rise, the
city can increase property taxes, which allows for
new streets, sidewalks, schools, bridges, etc. to be
built. This gives a slumping area (neighborhood)
a chance to improve the community by giving

residential and commercial grants to homeowners and business owners. People want to spend money in places where it seems like the business owners appreciate their customers and the only way to show your customers appreciation is by creating a clean, comfortable and accessible environment for the customer to enjoy and purchase your product or the products that your business offers. If you own a commercial property you want all your tenants to know that you appreciate your property by the way they are maintained. The better the property appearance the more money you are going to make. Keep your property in excellent condition so that their business is good and that allows you to collect rent on time and consistently. Marketing and advertising is a big part of letting people know about your business and what you are offering the people. Let the people know during your first encounter, what your business is. Give a short speech as you pass them your business card. Your business card should say everything that you do excellent in your business not all that you can do. There is a saying-jack of all trades and master of nothing. You do not need to have a core construction skill, but if you do, it can be your foundation to start your first project whether you do plumbing, heating and cooling, electrical and roofing cool. The contractor that does everything gets tired and burnt out doing everyone else's jobs and never completing the most important, your own projects that will give you the ultimate return on your time. People will always have work for a great contractor, but if you are trying to be an investor, boss or a real estate mogul you will not make it by fixing other people's property for them to sell. You need a TEAM that can help you generate that extra income from those customers construction jobs and not take away from your rehab project. Everything is about the strength of your TEAM in real estate investing. If your electrical man is incompetent then your property's electric will be bad and if your general contractor does not care about his position you will have trouble completing your rehab projects. It is all about your workers and your TEAM. The better your workers and your TEAM, the better your outcome of the project. A great

> *The contractor that does everything gets tired and burnt out never completing the most important, your own projects.*

TEAM that only knows a small amount of what to do but works together to find out the correct way to complete the project will give you a great result. A skilled TEAM with animosity anger and confrontation will ruin your project and burn your money up in bullshit work time! Bullshit work time is arguing for twenty minutes about how to do the job, then doing the job for an hour then arguing about another subject, sports, politics, or religion, then working for another hour (BSWT Bullshit Work Time). Never let anyone burn the clock on you, if you do happen to pay by the hour have someone make sure the work is being done. Your time is money. Pay for the job to be done, not for the time it takes the workers to do the job. Contract workers do the job for a set price opposed to an hourly wage from your TEAM which helps you and your business's profit margin. But make sure your TEAM still can eat with you or on another job!

CHANGING YOUR MIND

Every day you should wake and thank Your Higher Power. Say, "I deserve to win." I deserve to do better! **LAW 5 Change** How You Think In Order to **Change** How Your Life Is Going. If you are not where you want to be or if things are not going right most of the time you can look back on things

LAW 5
Change How You Think In Order to Change How Your Life Is Going.

that have happened bad or did not work out how you wanted them to. You can see that your thinking negative on anything over and over or questioning your set mind will cause the situation to end in a negative way or as you feared. We manifest that negativity into existence by thinking we do not deserve what it is that we are trying to get, by questioning our winning in life. We deserve to win. We all deserve greatness! It is just what you do with your

77

time and how much you persevere with passion and discipline. If you feel bad about what you want, you may bring those bad thoughts and feelings closer to you and manifest that negative energy into the reality of a bad situation. No one is perfect and not everything is going to go the way you want it to all the time, but with the proper preparation you will avoid a lot of problems. Knowing that negative thoughts produce negative outcomes will help you **Change Your Mind** and when you change your mind you change the way things in your life happen. Believe in yourself and the goals that you have set and move forward with the thoughts: "**This Is What I Deserve**" and "**I Should Be Winning In Life**". You and I have the same 24 hours in a day as Jay-Z, Oprah Winfrey, Warren Buffet, Bob Johnson and all the other people who are wealthy. We all have the resilience to do what we need to do to win and not what we want to do. It is what we do and what we think in our daily lives that separate us from our financial freedom. We have to train our minds and our hearts that we deserve the greatness that we are pursuing or have accomplished so that we can maintain the accomplished and keep moving forward towards our goal that we have set. Repairing your credit is as simple as you paying your debt or the bills you have accumulated throughout the course of your life, young or old. It could be college debt, credit cards you acquired while in college, or just every day bills. Whether they are late electric bills, car repossessions, or even foreclosures; it is all repairable. You can easily pay the bills by setting up pay arrangements or an agreement with the company that you may have debt with. Big or small, the company, nine times out of ten, will be willing to work with you to get the money you owe them, and you may also be able to pay a lower amount than what you actually owe. First, call the company and find out how much you owe and how much you can pay before you just send out a full balance check. It could be more or less than what your last statement may have displayed.

Another way to repair or improve your credit, is to dispute the bills that appear on your credit report. The credit bureaus will check with the company saying you owe the money and if they do not check back or answer the credit bureau, they will remove the fees owed. Many times companies go out of business, so the credit bureau may not receive a response and the debt is removed. This allows your credit score to improve. Credit affords you the opportunity to get or purchase things you can not really afford but may want and need. You will be able to access things that were once not available to you with credit. To eliminate the interest, you can pay double the amount of your bill every month and that will eliminate the interest that has been calculated for you to pay. Credit allows you to have things that you may not be able to afford right out but can pay off gradually until you own it. There are a number of credit repair companies that work from state to state that can help you repair your credit if you have any credit problems. There may also be non-profit or charitable organizations that may be willing and able to offer free assistance to repair your credit or even build your credit if you do not have a credit history established.

Contact the three credit bureaus at the following numbers:

Experian: (888) 397-3742
Equifax: (800) 846-5279
Transunion: (800) 916-8800

Property Purchase Price $25,000
Full Re-Hab Price $25,000
Property Sale Price $125,000 - $150,000
3 To 6 Months Repair Time

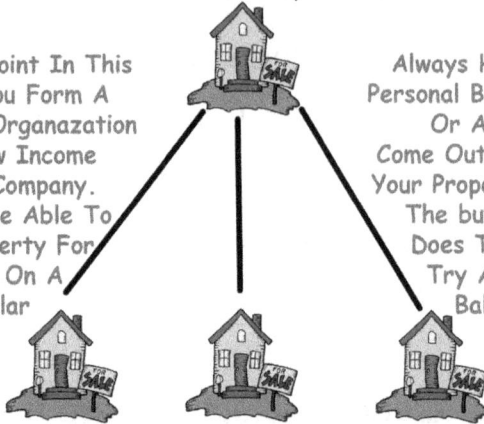

If At Any Point In This
Process You Form A
Non-Profit Organazation
501c3 Low Income
Housing Company.
You Will Be Able To
Buy Property For
Pennys On A
Dollar

Always Have Your
Personal Bank Apraiser
Or Apraiser
Come Out To Apraise
Your Property Before
The buyers Side
Does They May
Try And Low
Ball You

You Now Have $375,000 - $450,000 In Real Estate To Sell
$50,000 Get's You $125,000 - $150,000
$125,000 - $150,000 Gets You $375,000 - $450,000

6 Property's To Sell 3 To Rent
The Properties You Have Aquired Now Will Allow You
To Collect Rent For A Passive Income While Repairing
The Homes To Sell For The Larger Cash Flow.

HEALTH

◆ ◆ ◆

In order to enjoy your wealth, you have to have health. You have to have a good mind and body to enjoy the wealth you acquire throughout your life. The first thing I can give you as a gift of health is the Word "natural"! Natural is the kind of fruit and vegetables you want to eat. The more organic or natural foods you eat the better you do for your body. Natural foods are products that have undergone a minimum amount of processing or treatment with preservatives. The meat you eat also can be better than the regular beef, chicken, or fish that you are used to eating. I feel the health benefits are well worth the amount of money you spend. That extra couple of dollars you may spend will give you extra years on your life, a great trade. Another health benefit is working out running, pushups or swimming are all good for your body. You can not always look for the major work outs when you really want to do a few small exercises. Do what works for you and what your body and trainer say is correct. Do things to stay active like walk, run, ride a bike or jog. Anything to keep your blood circulating and the fresh air flowing through your lungs and your body in motion. Age creeps up on you before you know it. You have kids, gray hair, and grand kids to worry about. You want to be able to take time and enjoy your family, children and your wealth. If you truly want to enjoy life you have to live right. Food and exercise all matter when being healthy. Remember you can not enjoy the money you have accumulate if you are not healthy or alive once it has been made.

Editorial From: WTOP, Washington's Top News (www.wtop.com)

2019-20 Best Hospitals for Cardiology & Heart Surgery.

U.S. News evaluates hospitals performance in treating patients with challenging heart conditions such as advanced cardiovascular disease and other complex conditions. Hospitals are evaluated on 30-day survival; patient satisfaction; the proportion of patients who were discharged home after treatment (rather than going to another care facility); the quality and level of nurse staffing; advanced programs and technologies such as transplant programs; patient services such as cardiac rehabilitation and hospice; and other measures of care. Check out A Patient's Guide to Heart Disease to learn more about risk factors, symptoms and treatment options.

For children's hospitals, check out the Best Children's Hospitals for Pediatric Cardiology & Heart Surgery. You can also compare hospitals' performance in specific cardiac procedures such as abdominal aortic aneurysm repair, cardiac bypass surgery, congestive heart failure and aortic valve replacement surgery.

Here are the 10 top 2019-20 U.S. News Best Hospitals in the nation for Cardiology & Heart Surgery.

10. STANFORD HEALTH CARE-STANFORD HOSPITAL

Stanford Hospital in Palo Alto, California, comes in at No. 10 in the 2019-20 U.S. News Best Hospitals for Cardiology and Heart Surgery rankings.

9. BRIGHAM AND WOMEN'S HOSPITAL

Located in Boston, Brigham and Women's Hospital holds the ninth place in the 2019-20 Best Hospitals Cardiology & Heart Surgery rankings.

8. UCLA MEDICAL CENTER

UCLA Medical Center in Los Angeles claims the eighth place in the 2019-20 U.S. News Best Hospitals for Cardiology & Heart Surgery rankings.

7. NORTHWESTERN MEMORIAL HOSPITAL

Northwestern Memorial Hospital in Chicago takes the No. 7 spot in the U.S. News 2019-20

Best Hospitals for Cardiology & Heart Surgery
rankings.

6. MOUNT SINAI HOSPITAL

Mount Sinai Hospital in New York City claims the No. 6 place in the 2019-20 U.S. News Best Hospitals for Cardiology & Heart Surgery rankings.

5. MASSACHUSETTS GENERAL HOSPITAL

Massachusetts General Hospital in Boston is No. 5 in the 2019-20 Best Hospitals for Cardiology & Heart Surgery.

4. NEW YORK-PRESBYTERIAN HOSPITAL-COLUMBIA AND CORNELL

New York-Presbyterian Hospital in New York City comes in at No. 4 in Cardiology & Heart Surgery in the 2019-20 U.S. News Best Hospitals rankings.

3. CEDARS-SINAI MEDICAL CENTER

Cedars-Sinai Medical Center in Los Angeles claims the No. 3 title in the nation for Cardiology & Heart Surgery in the 2019-20 U.S. News Best Hospitals rankings.

2. MAYO CLINIC

Mayo Clinic, in Rochester, Minnesota, is the No. 2 hospital in the country for Cardiology & Heart Surgery in the 2019-20 U.S. News Best Hospitals rankings.

1. CLEVELAND CLINIC

The top hospital in the country for Cardiology & Heart Surgery in the 2019-20 U.S. Best Hospitals rankings is Cleveland Clinic.

Article from (www.entrepreneur.com) the editor: **Deep Patel** VIP CONTRIBUTOR Opinions expressed by *Entrepreneur* contributors are their own.

A new year brings new promise. It brings hope and, inevitably, a desire to better ourselves. In many ways, each new year is a fresh start and a chance to break old patterns and change unhealthy habits.

If January has given you a desire to improve your health and wellness, you've come to the right place. Harness that motivation and start making long-lasting, powerful changes that will improve your mental and physical health. Here are 10 keys to cultivating a healthier lifestyle for 2019 and beyond.

1. DITCH RESOLUTIONS.

The trouble with resolutions is that we often do not follow through and succeed with them. Why? Because a resolution is more like a temporary pledge -- you never really set up your lifestyle in a way that supports the change. Lasting success comes when you create habits that support the changes you want to see in your life. It means not giving up when you have a slip-up and sticking with it even during difficult, stressful times.

This year, be bold and ditch the New Year's resolution. Instead, use the momentum of the New Year to cultivate healthy habits that you can maintain for a lifetime. Building consistent, healthy habits is the key to lifelong well-being. After all, what we do every day matters more than what we do once in a while.

2. IDENTIFY THE AREAS YOU NEED TO STRENGTHEN FOR LONG-TERM HEALTH.

We all know we need to eat right, exercise, get plenty of sleep and drink lots of water in order to be healthy. Many of us think we're doing a decent job of being healthy. However, most of us are not. One study found that very few adults (only 3 percent) actually meet all the criteria of living a healthy lifestyle. Researchers looked at four keys to healthfulness, including:

- Not smoking.

- Maintaining a healthy weight (a BMI of 18-25), or successfully losing weight.

- Eating at least five servings of fruits and vegetables daily.

- Exercising 30 minutes or more, five times a week.

Few of us actually do all these things. And while these are important, there is more to good health than checking those boxes. It is also about having a positive attitude, a positive self-image, taking care of your mental health and spending time with friends and family. So, before you enter into a commitment to begin a healthier "you" in the New Year, decide which areas you desire to strengthen. Begin with your top one or two areas and work down your list.

3. KNOW WHAT WORKS FOR YOU.

Your ability to maintain a healthy lifestyle will depend on coming up with strategies that work with your personality. Take a moment to reflect on the times you succeeded and the times you struggled. What circumstances were most helpful to you and encouraged you to do your best?

What situations did you find distracting? What kept you from sticking with your goals? Whatever your goals are, before you can make changes to your lifestyle, you need to know where you are starting from and understand your reasons for making changes. Know what works for you and what doesn't.

4. DISRUPT AND CHANGE UNHEALTHY HABITS.

The things we do on a regular basis, from brushing our teeth to the snacks we reach for, often become our habits. The first step toward changing any behavior is to evaluate our current habits.

If you are in the habit of exercising every morning, that is good. If you are also in the habit of buying a bag of chips and a soda every afternoon, that is not. You need to look for ways to disrupt the patterns of unhealthy habits and establish new patterns, while continuing with your healthy habits. Start making small daily changes. Pack healthy snacks to take to work. Carry a refillable water bottle with you so you can stay hydrated throughout the day.

5. MAKE SMALL, POWERFUL CHANGES.

Do not try to make huge, sweeping life changes all at once. That can leave you feeling overwhelmed and tempted to give up altogether. Start small and build. If you are trying to get in the habit of working out more often but are out of shape and intimidated by the idea of exercise, start by doing the easiest, least-daunting exercise you can do. Try walking around the block for 10 minutes when you get home from work. Or even just doing a five-minute workout in your living room.

Whatever it is, start doing it on a daily basis. Once it feels like a normal part of your life, you can gradually increase it. If you have a setback, do not beat yourself up; just go back to doing what you were doing. The goal is to create habits that feel easy to achieve.

6. BUILD A LIFE THAT BLENDS WORK AND FUN.

Many successful entrepreneurs claim that work–life balance is a myth. The concept of finding balance often forces us to make concessions. We feel like we're in a huge juggling act, and we're left dizzy with obligations and stress. Instead, embrace the fact that work and life are often blurred. More and more, companies understand that we need to address life matters while at work and that we need flexibility in our work schedules.

The point is, instead of focusing on the boundaries where your work life ends and personal life begins, look for ways to blend the elements of your life. Focus on making consistent, healthy, positive choices that reflect your values, responsibilities and goals across all the aspects of life.

7. EAT A HEALTHY DIET.

As the saying goes, you are what you eat. The

meals and snacks we consume have a direct impact on our health. That doesn't mean you should skip exercise -- regular workouts will keep your metabolism revved up and help you burn fat. But you can't out-exercise a bad diet. A poor diet can cause a myriad of dire health problems, such as obesity, type 2 diabetes, heart disease and stroke, and these problems are increasingly being seen at a young age.

Even if you are a healthy weight, making sure you eat a nutritious diet is important to your long-term health. That means cutting back on sugar, boosting your intake of veggies and fruits, and avoiding processed "convenience" food. You do not have to give up all things yummy and fattening, but practice portion control.

8. GET ENOUGH QUALITY SLEEP.

Sometimes we overlook the importance of getting enough sleep. After all, if we're eating right, working out and avoiding bad habits like smoking, does it really matter if we're getting the recommended 8 hours of sleep a night? It sure does! Sleep plays a vital role in our health and well-being through our lives.

Getting enough quality sleep aids in both mental and physical health. Sleep is key to brain function -- it affects how well you learn, work, think, react and get along with others. Having an ongoing sleep deficiency raises your risk for chronic health problems. During the day, your body gets broken down by your environment and the tasks you perform. Sleep restores you. Make sure you make sleep a cornerstone of your new healthy lifestyle.

9. MANAGE STRESS.

Our world requires us to live in a highly active and pressurized environment. Activities in our lives occur so fast it is often a struggle to keep up.

This causes stress to accumulate. It is important that we distinguish between the things that are within our control and the things that aren't. For example, getting a flat tire is out of your control, but getting a bad review for mediocre work is within your control.

You can reduce and manage your stress by taking control of the things you can control. This way, when unexpected stressful events occur, you will be relaxed enough to focus on them and solve those problems without becoming overwhelmed. You can also engage in relaxing therapies such as meditation and breathing deeply to help you manage feelings of stress.

10. SLOW DOWN AND REFLECT ON THE MOMENT.

Many of us are so focused on our jobs and everyday tasks that we forget to enjoy the moment we are experiencing. Pause throughout your day and appreciate the beauty of the world around you, the sound of laughter, how the sun feels on your face, how your legs feel as you walk. Make time to enjoy each part of your day, and then step back and enjoy the process you are a part of. The business world is systematic and requires constant innovation and analysis -- it is focused on the final product. Learn to enjoy each step of this process. Doing so will contribute to your product's overall success, and will make the final outcome much more enjoyable.

I enjoyed this article so I wanted to share it with my readers. "I think Deep Patel makes valid points throughout the article"

BASIC RENTAL AGREEMENT OR RESIDENTIAL LEASE

This Rental Agreement or Residential Lease shall evidence the complete terms and conditions under which the parties whose signatures appear below have agreed. Landlord, _____, shall be referred to as "OWNER" and Tenant(s) _____, shall be referred to as "RESIDENT." As consideration for this agreement, OWNER agrees to rent/lease to RESIDENT and RESIDENT agrees to rent/lease from OWNER for use solely as a private residence, the premises located at _____ in the city of _____ .

1. **TERMS:** RESIDENT agrees to pay in advance $_____ per month on the ____ day of each month.

2. **LATE CHARGE:** A late fee of $_____, shall be added and due for any payment of rent made after the _____ of the month. Any dishonored check shall be treated as unpaid rent, and subject to an additional fee of $_____ .

3. **UTILITIES:** RESIDENT agrees to pay all utilities and/or services based upon occupancy of the premises except _____ .

4. **OCCUPANTS:** Guest(s) staying over 15 days without the written consent of OWNER shall be considered a breach of this agreement. ONLY the following individuals and/or animals, AND NO OTHERS shall occupy the subject residence for more than 15 days unless the expressed written consent of OWNER obtained in advance _____ .

5. **PETS:** No animal, fowl, fish, reptile, and/or pet of any kind shall be kept on or about the premises, for any amount of time, without obtaining the prior written consent and meeting the requirements of the OWNER. Such consent if granted, shall be revocable at OWNER'S option upon giving a 30 day written notice. In the event laws are passed or permission is granted to have a pet and/or animal of any kind, an additional deposit in the amount of $_____ shall be required along with additional monthly rent of $_____ along with the signing of OWNER'S Pet Agreement. RESIDENT also agrees to carry insurance deemed appropriate by OWNER to cover possible liability and damages that may be caused by such animals.

6. **NOISE:** RESIDENT agrees not to cause or allow any noise or activity on the premises which might disturb the peace and quiet of another RESIDENT and/or neighbor. Said noise and/or activity shall be a breach of this agreement.

7. **DESTRUCTION OF PREMISES:** If the premises become totally or partially destroyed during the term of this Agreement so that RESIDENT'S use is seriously impaired, OWNER or RESIDENT may terminate this Agreement immediately upon three day written notice to the other.

8. **CONDITION OF PREMISES:** RESIDENT acknowledges that he has examined the premises and that said premises, all furnishings, fixtures, furniture, plumbing, heating, electrical facilities, all items listed on the attached property condition checklist, if any, and/or all other items provided by OWNER are all clean, and in good satisfactory condition except as may be indicated elsewhere in this Agreement. RESIDENT agrees to keep the premises and all items in good order and good condition and to immediately pay for costs to repair and/or replace any portion of the above damaged by RESIDENT, his guests and/or invitees, except as provided by law. At the termination of this Agreement, all of above items in this provision shall be returned to OWNER in clean and good condition except for reasonable wear and tear and the premises shall be free of all personal property

NOTEWORTHY QUOTES

$\bullet\ \blacklozenge\ \bullet$

"A funny thing happens in real estate. When it comes back, it comes back up like gangbusters." - **Barbara Corcoran**, real estate investor

"To be successful in real estate, you must always and consistently put your clients' best interests first. When you do, your personal needs will be realized beyond your greatest expectations." -- **Anthony Hitt**, real estate professional

"Games are won by players who focus on the playing field—not by those whose eyes are glued to the scoreboard. If you instead focus on the prospective price change of a contemplated purchase, you are speculating. There is nothing improper about that. I know, however, that I am unable to speculate successfully, and I am skeptical of those who claim sustained success at doing so." - **Warren Buffett**, billionaire investor

"It is a comfortable feeling to know that you stand on your own ground. Land is about the only thing that can't fly away." -- **Anthony Trollope**, novelist

"The best investment on Earth is earth." - **Louis Glickman**, real estate investor

"In my experience, in the real-estate business past success stories are generally not applicable to new situations. We must continually reinvent ourselves, responding to changing times with innovative new business models." - **Akira Mori**, real estate developer

"I have always liked real estate; farm land, pasture land, timber land and city property. I have had experience with all of them. I guess I just naturally like 'the good Earth,' the foundation of all our wealth." - **Jesse Jones**, entrepreneur

"In the real estate business, you learn more about people, and you learn more about life, you learn more about the impact of government, probably than any other profession that I know of." **Johnny Isakson**, U.S. Senator "

"Some people look for a beautiful place, others make a beautiful place." **Hazrat Inayat Khan**, spiritualist

"Real Estate cannot be lost or stolen, nor can it be carried away. Purchased with common sense, paid for in full, and managed with reasonable care, it is about the safest investment in the world." – **Franklin D Roosevelt**, U.S. President

"Ninety percent of all millionaire become so through owning real estate. More money has been made in real estate than in all industrial investments combined. The wise Young men are wage earner of today invests his money in real estate." **Andrew Carnegie**, billionaire industrialist

"In the real estate business, you learn more about people, and you learn more about life, you learn more about the impact of government, probably than any other profession that I know of." **Johnny Isakson**, U.S. Senator

"Buy land, they're not making it anymore." **Mark Twain**, writer & humorist

"Landlords grow rich in their sleep without working, risking or economizing." **John Stuart Mill**, political economist

"A Happy Family Is But A Early Heaven" **George Bernard Shaw**

"If a man breaks a pledge, the public ought to know it." **Steve Forbes**

"I Didn't Quit I Just Ran Out Of Gas For A Moment." **Robert Pyles**, investor

Worry is the most useless human activity on earth... All it changes is your blood pressure. Use your energy to plan the future. **Myles Munroe**

Walk by faith not by sight is my motto. Don't ask for it, work for it. **@Kustoo** (Instagram)

I always say... In order to be successful in business and life you have to becomfortable with having uncomfortable conversations. **@patrickcapttalgroup**(Instagram)

WORDS TO KNOW

◆ ◆ ◆

Mortgage – The legal documents that oblige you to pay for the property over a certain length of time constitute your mortgage. The property itself secures the loan. When you sell your house, you must pay off the mortgage. The new owner will obtain his own financing.

Title – A title is a listing of the history of owners, debts, and other information related to your house. Title is produced by researching the documents recorded in the land records of your county. If you have multiple liens and mortgages on your property, selling a home and transferring the title to new owners can be complex.

Disclosures – You must state the condition of the property as you know it. The regulations about what must be disclosed vary by state, but issues such as water damage or a leaky roof should usually be mentioned to potential buyers. If you are not in a position to repair problems, you should at least put them on the table, so the buyer can decide whether he/she wants to take them on.

Price – The amount of value in terms of money at which property is offered for sale or is exchanged for at a sale. Often, there is a discrepancy between the price which the house is listed and the selling price. Setting the price at a level that considers its value and those of comparable properties in the neighborhood can bridge the gap.

Appraisal – A third party evaluator examines the property to determine that the price is in line with comparable properties. If the appraisal comes in too low, the lender will either refuse to write the loan or request that the buyer contribute more down payment.

Equity – The amount of financial interest the home-owner invests in the property is considered equity. Equity can be calculated by subtracting your mort-gage balance from the current market value of the home. If the value of your home has decreased, you could be in a negative equity position. The amount of equity you have might influence your decision to sell a home.

Underwater mortgage – If you owe more on your home than it is currently worth, your mortgage is considered "underwater." If you sell a home for less than you owe, you may have to pay your lender the difference.

Short sale – If the lender agrees to accept less than the amount owed on the mortgage, the property can be sold at short sale. The process can be lengthy in addition to the normal negotiation between yourself and the buyer, the lender determines what amount they will accept.

Foreclosure – If the borrower can't pay the mortgage, the lender can begin court proceedings to rescind his interest in the property. If the property is sold at auction, the proceeds are applied towards the mortgage.

Quitclaim deed - A quitclaim deed is a legal instrument that is used to transfer interest in real property. The entity transferring its interest is called the grantor, and when the quitclaim deed is properly completed and executed, it transfers any interest the grantor has in the property to a recipient, called the grantee.

Real Estate Agent – An individual who is licensed to negotiate and transact the real estate sales.

Real Property – Land and anything else of a permanent nature that is affixed to the land.

Realtor – A real estate agent or broker who is an active member of a local real estate board affiliated with the national association of realtors.

Refinance Transaction – The act of paying off an existing loan using the funding gained from a new loan which uses the sane property as security.

Real Estate Investment Trust (REIT) – A trust corporation that combines the capital of several investors for the purpose of acquiring or providing funding for real estate.

Return on Assets – The measurement of money that has been gained as a result of certain investments.

Revolving Debt – A logical approach to analyzing and defining insurable and non-insurable risk while evaluating the availability and cost of purchasing third-party insurance.

Sales Contract – An Agreement that both the buyer and seller sign defining the terms of a property sale.

Seller Financing - A type of funding in which the borrower may use part of the equity in the property to finance the purchase.

Subcontractor – A contractor who has been hired by the general contractor, often specializing in a certain required task for the construction project.

Tax Lien – A type of lien placed against a property if the owner has not paid property or personal taxes.

TIME

◆ ◆ ◆

LAW 5 Is a life and business law, it is to be mindful of your time, time management is everything. You need time for so many things; time for work time for play, time to plan, time to eat, time to sleep, and time to be with your family. Everything needs time, but you have to find a way to manage

◆ ◆ ◆
LAW 5
Be mindful of your time.

your time correctly and not all things may be equally matched with time. There are two things you can not lack on with time and that is your family time and your health time. No one wants to be rich and lonely, not having family and people you love and care about around. And you do not want to have money but always at the doctor because on your way to wealth you forgot about your health. You have to give your business a lot of time almost as much as your health. You may still have a job that you work for eight hours a day. How do you fit it all in? You have to find a way.

Make your family part of your business, meaning take your kids with you on your job site or to your business or the company you own. Include your significant other or girlfriend to see if she believes in your vision before you commit. That will help in determining if you want her as your wife from a girlfriend, maybe or maybe not. You do not want to waste time on someone that does not support your vision, that is growing and has a solid foundation for growth. Life is harder when you have people around that can not see your vision or you choose the wrong partner that just does not want to support what you are doing. I have had support and I have had no support from a person I was in a relationship with. It feels much better to come home from working hard to talk with someone that will take the time to listen and understand that everyday is different and that business is sometimes stressful! There are numerous ways that can help you not worry about needing help in the future from anyone. To flourish and grow your business, peace of mind is everything. Being able to take the time and think is priceless. Time management in life is essential. In a matter of seconds a man or woman can make a split second decision to commit an action and in those few seconds of time life can change for years to come in the future in a negative way or a positive way. Negative being debt, loss a jail sentence, pain, or regret. Positive being wealth, health, happiness, great memories, good business and the option of time. Time is everything for everyone. We all have the same 24 hours in a day as the people we call stars or mentors, the ones thriving in their greatness or business. So why not you, why not your family. How can you manage time in your areas of greatness? You have to want it as much as you say and put in relentless effort to get what it is you say you want to achieve. Everything in life takes time. Sometimes the time will be short and sometimes it will take longer. The amount of time your goal or achievement takes is on you and your dedication to that goal or achievement. A relentless effort to gain knowledge in the area of real estate and investing in it is what lead me to understand my greatness and what I needed to do with my time. It was simply said to me from an excellent friend and mentor Robert Pyles, "stop and look at what it is that has always given you reward and a check when you put in the time and has never failed you". It was real estate. I gave my time to what has never failed me. I put the time and skill in needed to repair my properties to flip and sell for a profit, and my property portfolio grew along with my bank account.

INCREASE YOUR PROPERTIES VALUE

◆ ◆ ◆

There are more than three ways to gain value in a property. I think three of the best ways to increase your properties value in the first year of ownership is to, one, do bathroom repairs: change the toilet and the sink and shower fixtures and the vanity if possible. If you can put in new tile backing in the shower and ceramic tile on the floor; two, kitchen repairs; or three, add addition if possible. The kitchen being the place you spend a large amount of time cooking, eating or preparing a snack or a meal. You may invite company over and they will be happy to eat lunch in your kitchen area without a thought except, how much does something like this cost. The third way to add value to your single family flip is to finish the basement. Lower level living is what you want to offer the buyer. This is another way to add additional space to your property without building an addition on to the home. A finished basement with an egress window for an easy fire exit in case of an emergency. You want to give the people living in the lower level a safe way out if there was a problem on the upper levels of the home. Finishing the basement and adding an egress window will give your house a value like no other home in the area because of the extra living space you have created. The space can be for an older child or visiting family members or even a rental unit if allowed in your city or state that your property is in. Remember never cut corners and buy cheap light fixture or cheap carpet like someone would use in a rental unit. This property will be someone's home. Give the home buyer something to feel excellent about and fall in love with. Buy great lights and great bathroom and kitchen water fixtures. Wow the potential buyer from the minute he or she walks in the property.

Property That Have Been Repaired and Sold by NYCINC & Diverse Community Investments LLC

26th & Hampton

SOLD $15,000.00

2109 – 11 W McKinley

SOLD $135,000.00

24th & McKinley

SOLD $45,000.00

4715 – 19 West Center St.

SOLD $80,000.00

1514 West Burleigh

SOLD $10,000.00

4116 North 26th Street

SOLD
$16,000.00

4326 N 28th Street

SOLD $17,500.00

408 East North Ave
Owned Free & Clear

97-07 32nd Ave, East Elmherst, Qu, NY 11369
$660,000

RENT RECEIPT

NAME AND/
OR ADDRESS

DATE   /   /

☐ CASH ☐ CHECK # _____ ☐ MONEY ORDER # _____

SIGNATURE

AMOUNT $ _____ . ‾100‾

MEMO

© 2008 ezLandlordForms

RENT RECEIPT

NAME AND/
OR ADDRESS

DATE   /   /

☐ CASH ☐ CHECK # _____ ☐ MONEY ORDER # _____

SIGNATURE

AMOUNT $ _____ . ‾100‾

MEMO

© 2008 ezLandlordForms

RENT RECEIPT

NAME AND/
OR ADDRESS

DATE   /   /

☐ CASH ☐ CHECK # _____ ☐ MONEY ORDER # _____

SIGNATURE

AMOUNT $ _____ . ‾100‾

MEMO

© 2008 ezLandlordForms

RENT RECEIPT

NAME AND/
OR ADDRESS

DATE   /   /

☐ CASH ☐ CHECK # _____ ☐ MONEY ORDER # _____

SIGNATURE

AMOUNT $ _____ . ‾100‾

MEMO

© 2008 ezLandlordForms

I WOULD BE A REAL-ESTATE INVESTOR BUT_____!

DOUBLE

$1000

$2000

$4000

$8000

$16,000

$32,000

$64,000

$128,000

$256,000

$512,000

$1,024,000

$2,048,000

$4,096,000

Whatever works for you, double your money and do not look back. Invest in you. Do not let anyone steal your dream protect your ideas like it is your wife or your life. Real estate works for me when it comes to doubling my money. If I buy a property for $35,000.00 ($20,000.00 to purchase

& $15,000.00 - $20,000.00 for repairs) totaling $35,000.00 - $40,000.00 that house will sell for $65,000.00 - $75,000.00 if not more, period. Remember know what houses are selling for (comping for) in your investment area so that your guaranteed your sale price. You know what brings value to the property and you make those repairs for the property to be listed and sold.

There's

Money

In

That

House

Reference Page

Basic Rental Agreement - Google
Blank Rent Reciept - Google
Property Repair Checklist - Google
www.Biography.com Pages -14, 15, 16, 17, 18, 19.
Google / Yahoo Pages - 56, 57, 58, 59, 60, 61, 62.
Webster Dictionary Pages - 66, 67, Listen, Learn and Lead.
Google - 62, 63, 64, 65, 66, 67, 68.
Google / Yahoo Pages - 97, 98, 99, 100.
www.usa.gov
www.wdfi.org
www.hud.gov
www.census.gov
www.wtop.com
www.fittedsole.com
www.newyoungcreators.com
Article From (www.entrepreneur.com) Editor: Deep Patel Pages - 87
88, 89, 90, 91, 92, 93, 94, 95,
Editor & Vectoring - Gretchen Kletzien
Copy Editor - Jane Kirkwood
Art - Jordan Johnson
Sports Car Art Page - 72, Google Free Art
Fact-Checker Kayla Davis

www.ingramcontent.com/pod-product-compliance
Lightning Source LLC
Chambersburg PA
CBHW060615210326
41520CB00010B/1344